KIDS' BOOK OF
Quotes from the African American Tradition

compiled by Cheryl and Wade Hudson
Pictures by Anna Rich

Kids' Book of Wisdom: Quotes from the African American Tradition

Ccpyright 1996 by JUST US BOOKS, INC.
Introduction copyright 1996 by Cheryl and Wade Hudson.
Illustrations copyright 1996 by Anna Rich.

Printed in the USA/First Edition 10 9 8 7 6 5 4 3 2 1
Library of Congress Catalog Number 96-76533
ISBN: 0-940975-61-0

JUST US BOOKS
East Orange, NJ

INTRODUCTION

Wit and wisdom from the African American experience are to be cherished and celebrated. Within them lie the creativity, understanding, strength and courage of a people who have been able not only to endure, but to thrive under extremely difficult conditions. These quotes, proverbs and sayings, many of which have been passed down from generation to generation, still empower, enrich, and are a source of inspiration for many of us today.

There are many books that have been published in recent years that make wisdom from the African American tradition accessible. There are, however, very few that have been written specifically for our youth.

Wisdom from the African American tradition is a power source for all of us.

Our hope is that <u>Kids' Book of Wisdom</u> will help young people understand that. They can be empowered by the connection.

CH & WH

Contents

AMBITION

ambition: a strong desire to gain a particular objective; the drive to succeed.

Ambition is another way of saying you must really want to achieve the goal you have set. The drive to succeed will help you endure hard work and make the sacrifices that are required to reach your goal.

Dr. Mae Jemison's ambition helped her become the first Black woman astronaut. She really wanted to fly in outer space. Michael Jordan wanted to be a great basketball player. So he sometimes practiced until late in the evening after the other players had quit. Ambition helped both of these people to achieve their goals. It will help you, too.

The sun cannot be hidden.
— *Egypt*

Every dog has its day.
—*Traditional*

A man with too much ambition cannot
sleep in peace.
—*Baguirmi*

Our children must never lose their zeal for
building a better world.
— *Mary McLeod Bethune*

The son of a fool will not become a chief.
— *Kunama*

3

I rise above myself/
like a fish flying.
— *Lucille Clifton*
Good News About the Earth

Humility is the crown of virtue.
— *Egypt*

It's a po' dog that don't wag his own tail.
—*Traditional*

I know that I can only get into the sunlight
by work and only remain there by more work.
— *Zora Neale Hurston, 1925*

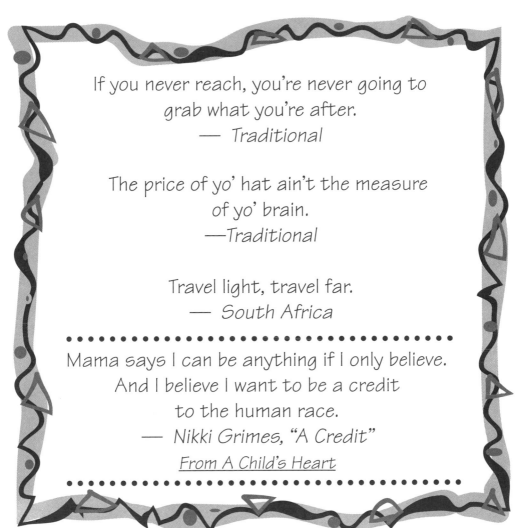

If you never reach, you're never going to
grab what you're after.
— *Traditional*

The price of yo' hat ain't the measure
of yo' brain.
—*Traditional*

Travel light, travel far.
— *South Africa*

Mama says I can be anything if I only believe.
And I believe I want to be a credit
to the human race.
— *Nikki Grimes, "A Credit"*
From A Child's Heart

COOPERATION

cooperation: a joint effort; a group of people working together for a common purpose.

Many important goals in life cannot be achieved by one person acting alone. Reaching these goals requires the help of others who are willing to do their part.

One player cannot win a baseball game. It takes nine players working as a whole.

A family is a team, too. Each member has a part to play to make the family the best it can be. To cooperate, you must be willing to work with others.

If you are in one boat you have to row together.
—*South Africa*

It takes a whole village to raise a child.
—*West Africa*

We are one, our cause is one, and we
must help each other if we are to succeed.
—*Frederick Douglass, 1847*

If the fingers of one hand quarrel,
they cannot pick up the food.
—*East Africa*

You can lead a horse to water, but you can't
make him drink.
—*Traditional*

Each one teach one.
Each one reach one.
—*Civil Rights Movement*

Let the elephant fell the trees,
Let the bushpig dig the holes,
Let the mason wasp fill in the walls,
Let the giraffe put up the roof,
Then we'll have a house.
—*Zaire*

Let nothing and nobody break your spirit.
Let the unity in the community remain in tact.
—*Jesse Jackson*

Even the sharpest knife-blade cannot carve
its own handle.
—*Anonymous*

We can all sing together, but we
can't all talk together.
——*Traditional*

You have to take the fat with the lean.
——*Traditional*

Little by little the cotton thread
becomes a loincloth.
——*Benin*

• •

After supper Jamal started washing dishes
because it was his turn. That's the way they
did things. One day Mama washed the dishes,
one day Sassy did them, and then Jamal.
——*Walter Dean Myers*
Scorpions

• •

9

COURAGE & STRENGTH

courage: a quality that makes it possible for a person to face danger or difficulties without fear.

strength: the power to withstand or resist attack, force, strain, or stress without breaking or yielding.

Fear often keeps us from doing what we have to if we are to succeed. Courage keeps us going.

Dr. Martin Luther King, Jr. continued to lead the struggle for human rights and justice even though he faced death almost every day. Death threats did not stop Malcolm X either. Why were these two men able to stand tall in the face of danger? They both had courage. Courage helped them overcome the fear that could have stopped them from doing what they had to do. Strength, especially inner strength, kept them from giving up or cracking under the constant pressure they faced.

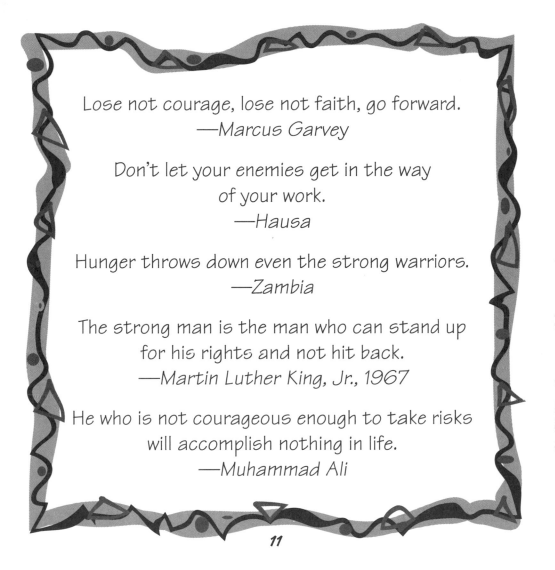

Lose not courage, lose not faith, go forward.
—Marcus Garvey

Don't let your enemies get in the way
of your work.
—Hausa

Hunger throws down even the strong warriors.
—Zambia

The strong man is the man who can stand up
for his rights and not hit back.
—Martin Luther King, Jr., 1967

He who is not courageous enough to take risks
will accomplish nothing in life.
—Muhammad Ali

If he wasn't a coward, he wouldn't gang up on you.
—*Malcolm X, 1965*

If you have never been sick, you boast
of your strength.
—*Traditional*

Strategy is better than strength.
—*Hausa*

• •

"Gather up your courage. Fight, Jacob.
Fight off the flames of all those bad feelings
you carry inside. Believe in your strength.
Believe in your love for your brother.
Believe that you can save Peewee—and you will!"
—*Phil Mendez, The Black Snowman*

• •

When spider webs unite,
they can tie up a lion.
—*Ethiopia*

Take courage my soul, and let me journey on.
For the night is dark and I am far from home.
Thanks be to God, the morning light appears.
The storm is passing over...Hallelujah!
—Lyrics, *Black Spiritual*

••

Believing in yourself takes courage.
Facing the future takes hope.
Carry both in your heart.
—*Rosa Parks, 1995*
<u>Dear Mrs. Parks: A Dialogue with Today's Youth</u>

••

CREATIVITY & IMAGINATION

creativity: the ability to produce by one's own intelligence, imagination, or skill.

imagination: the act or power of forming images in the mind of things that are not actually present.

We all have the ability to be creative. We must, however, be willing to let our imagination soar, and put our skills to work.

Imagination is a very important part of creativity. Many of the useful tools, machines, and artifacts we value today came about because of the imagination of those who created them.

Before Garrett Morgan could use his creativity to invent the traffic light, he had to use his imagination to see it in his mind. Your creativity can help you accomplish great things.

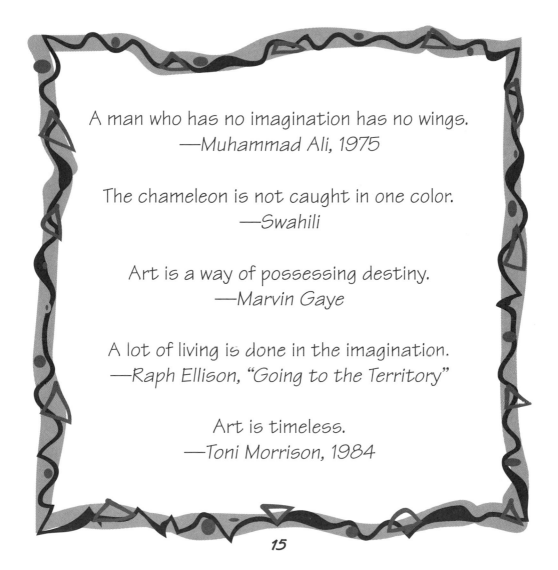

A man who has no imagination has no wings.
—Muhammad Ali, 1975

The chameleon is not caught in one color.
—Swahili

Art is a way of possessing destiny.
—Marvin Gaye

A lot of living is done in the imagination.
—Raph Ellison, "Going to the Territory"

Art is timeless.
—Toni Morrison, 1984

I can make something out of the children...
they have the essence of greatness in them.
—Zora Neale Hurston, _Moses, Man of the Mountain_

Create and be true to yourself, and
depend only on your own good taste.
—Duke Ellington, _Music is My Mistress_

Art is not simply works of art; it has the
spirit that knows beauty, that has music in
its soul and the color of sunsets in its
handkerchief, that can dance on a flaming
world and make the world dance too.
—W.E.B. DuBois, _The Souls of Black Folk_

I just can't stay still when the music
sweets me so.
—Ashley Bryan, _The Dancing Granny_

Thoughts are free: no one can read them
or steal them.
—South Africa

This lil' light of mine
I'm gonna let it shine.
—Spiritual

It is good to know truth, but it is better
to speak of palm trees.
—West Africa

daddy says the world is / a drum
tight and hard / and I told him
i'm gonna beat / out my own rhythm
—Nikki Giovanni, "the drum"
Spin A Soft Black Song

DISCIPLINE

discipline: self control or orderly conduct;
the ability to control one's actions or emotions.

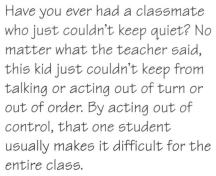

Have you ever had a classmate who just couldn't keep quiet? No matter what the teacher said, this kid just couldn't keep from talking or acting out of turn or out of order. By acting out of control, that one student usually makes it difficult for the entire class.

More than likely that student lacks self-discipline.

Discipline helps you to control your emotions and act in an orderly way. Without discipline it is difficult to reach your goals.

18

Do not try your luck once.
Try it again and again.
—*Zande*

Be responsible for (your) actions
and take responsible actions.
—*Haki R. Madhubuti, 1975*

The son who is too lazy to help his father
in the fields, will starve when his father
has worked himself to death.
—*Tanzania*

You cannot take medicine for someone else.
—*Tanzania*

It doesn't matter what you are trying to accomplish. It's all a matter of discipline.
—Wilma Rudolph

Where two quarrel, two are guilty.
—South Africa

If you threaten to punish your child, do it or else he will not respect you.
—Ghana

Don't pat the cow before you milk her.
—Hausa

Better mind that sun, and see how she run. And don't let him catch you with your work undone.
—Blues Lyrics

If you are building a house and a nail breaks,
do you stop building, or do you change the nail?
—Kwanda Burundi

If you learn it while young, you can do it when old.
—South Africa

The one who itches is the one who scratches.
—Tanzania

• •

Sis always says,/ "If you're gonna do something,
do it right." /So when I do my homework every
night, /I draw my letters straight and neat in my
notebook. /I know the teacher may not take the
time to look, /but Sis says do it anyway, even if
nobody else can see—/except You, Lord, and me.
Nikki Grimes, "Big Sister Says"
<u>From A Child's Heart</u>

• •

FRIENDS & FAMILY

friend: someone a person likes and is fond of;
someone who is reliable and supportive.

family: a group of people connected by blood or marriage.

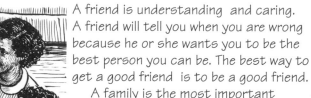

A friend is understanding and caring. A friend will tell you when you are wrong because he or she wants you to be the best person you can be. The best way to get a good friend is to be a good friend.

A family is the most important group to which most of us will ever belong. It is not just a mother, father, and children, but includes aunts, uncles, grandparents, and cousins.

A good family provides love and support. It makes us feel safe and secure. Those who come from supportive and loving families usually feel good about themselves. They have positive attitudes about life. Every member of a family is important.

If you have friends you will not be alone.
—*Yaunde*

A friend is the one who praises you
when you are not there.
—*Yoruba*

The tree cannot live without its branches.
—*Namibia*

Everybody that grins in your face
ain't no friend to you.
—*Traditional*

A brother is like one's shoulder.
—*Somalia*

You never miss the water till the well goes dry.
You'll never miss your baby till she says good-bye.
—*Blues lyrics*

Jay-bird don't rob his own nest.
—*Traditional*

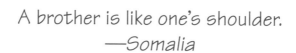

A friend is like a crown of rubies, beautiful
and rare. You're the most precious jewel of all,
the one, the only Amir. With all my love,
Doris
—*Joyce Hansen, <u>Yellow Bird and Me</u>*

None but a mule deserves his family.
—Africa

When you follow in the path of your father,
you learn to walk like him.
—Ashanti

••

Mattie looked out at them. I have made a place
for myself in the circle of my family, she thought.
It is still a bumpy circle and maybe Matt will
always be Mama's favorite, but that's okay.
At least I have a place with Mama.
—Candy Dawson Boyd, _Circle of Gold_

••

INDEPENDENCE & SELF DETERMINATION

independence: the state or quality of being independent (not easily influenced or controlled by others; self-reliant)

self determination: the right of a person to decide what is best without outside influences

Peer pressure often makes us follow others. Too often, however, following others may get us into trouble. It is important that we learn to be independent and to make our own decisions. Getting advice from those we trust is very helpful in making us confident in ourselves and our ability to make good decisions. Self-determination helps us define ourselves and helps to put control of our lives in our own hands.

The tortoise is the wisest.
He carries his own home.
—*Bambara*

Character, not circumstances make the man.
—*Booker T. Washington*

Mama may have. /Papa may have.
But God bless the child that's got his own.
—*Billie Holiday*
"God Bless the Child"

One bracelet does not rattle.
—*Tetela*

Even the tiny ant has a home of his own.
—*North Africa*

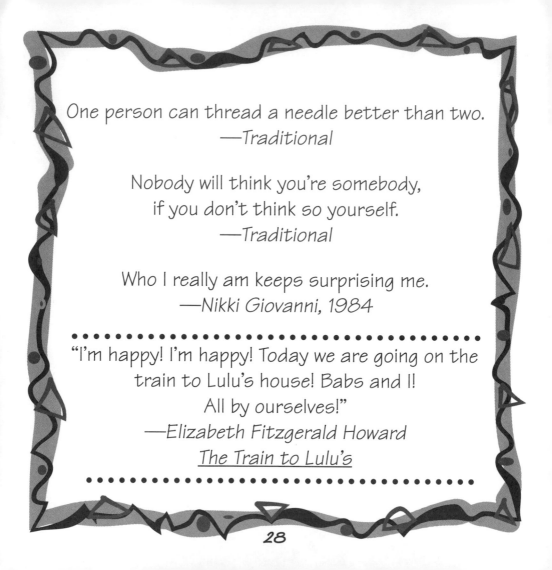

One person can thread a needle better than two.
—*Traditional*

Nobody will think you're somebody,
if you don't think so yourself.
—*Traditional*

Who I really am keeps surprising me.
—*Nikki Giovanni, 1984*

"I'm happy! I'm happy! Today we are going on the
train to Lulu's house! Babs and I!
All by ourselves!"
—Elizabeth Fitzgerald Howard
<u>The Train to Lulu's</u>

The ole sheep, they know the road;
young lambs gotta find the way.
—*Blues lyrics*

No one can travel by someone else's star.
—*Swahili*

A leopard can't change its spots.
—*Traditional*

It's nature's nice decree that tiger folks should
be not dainty, but daring, and wisely wearing
what's fierce as the face.
Not whiteness and lace!
—*Gwendolyn Brooks*
The Tiger Who Wore White Gloves

KINDNESS & LOVE

kindness: possessing the quality to be gentle, considerate and friendly toward others.

love: a strong feeling of affection, devotion and concern for another person.

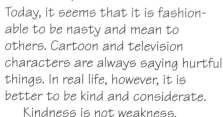

Today, it seems that it is fashionable to be nasty and mean to others. Cartoon and television characters are always saying hurtful things. In real life, however, it is better to be kind and considerate.

Kindness is not weakness. Kindness shows that we care and respect others. Love is one of the strongest feelings we can have. Love expresses itself in many ways. When we love someone, we are concerned about what happens to that person. We respect him or her. When we love others, we also feel good about ourselves.

Kindness is the best remedy for suffering.
—*Mozambique*

Love is the most durable power in the world.
This creative force is the most potent
instrument available in mankind's quest
for peace and security.
—*Martin Luther King, Jr., <u>Strength to Love</u>*

God returns the good that one does.
—*West Africa*

Love is like seed.
It does not choose the ground on which it falls.
—*Zulu*

Ashes fly back into the face of
he who throws them.
—*Niger*

It is better to be loved than feared.
—*Senegal*

The lessons of all the ages upon this point
is that a wrong done to one man
is a wrong done to all men.
—*Frederick Douglass,*
<u>*The Life and Times of Frederick Douglass*</u>

Love is in need of love today/
Don't delay/Send yours right away.
—*Stevie Wonder*
"Love's In Need of Love Today"

Do not be like the mosquito that
bites the owner of the house.
—Malawi

Tell me whom you love, I'll tell you who you are.
—Creole proverb

There is always something left to love. And if
you ain't learned that, you ain't learned nothing.
—Lorraine Hansberry

● ●

I asked Mama,
"What will you put in the basket, Mama?"
And she said, "I think I'll put love."
—Camille Yarbrough
Cornrows

● ●

KNOWLEDGE & WISDOM

knowledge: what is known from understanding, experience, study or awareness.

wisdom: the quality of being wise; power of judging rightly and following the soundest course of action based on knowledge, experience and understanding.

We sometimes think that only senior citizens have wisdom. It is true that wisdom comes with age. But having wisdom involves more than living a long time and having had many life experiences. Wisdom also means showing good judgment, and having the ability to use our knowledge and experiences wisely.

We should learn to appreciate all that we learn. Knowledge is very important. Whether through study, experience, or understanding, the knowledge that we acquire prepares us for a richer and more fulfilling life.

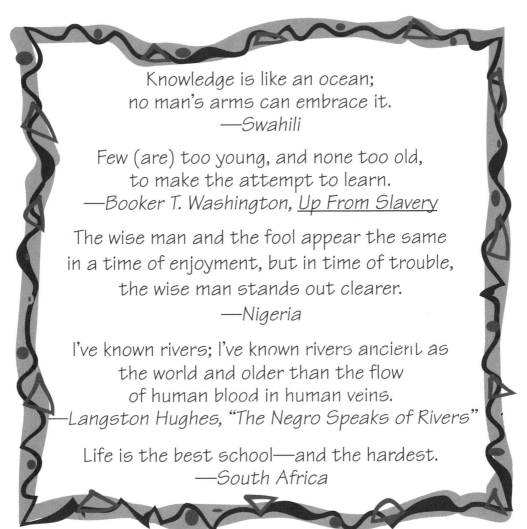

Knowledge is like an ocean;
no man's arms can embrace it.
—Swahili

Few (are) too young, and none too old,
to make the attempt to learn.
—Booker T. Washington, _Up From Slavery_

The wise man and the fool appear the same
in a time of enjoyment, but in time of trouble,
the wise man stands out clearer.
—Nigeria

I've known rivers; I've known rivers ancient as
the world and older than the flow
of human blood in human veins.
—Langston Hughes, "The Negro Speaks of Rivers"

Life is the best school—and the hardest.
—South Africa

The hunter knows the language of the animals.
—Mozambique

The giraffe is wise; he never makes a noise
but he can see far away.
—Tanzania

When two quarrel, the first to stop is the wisest.
—South Africa

• •

I am 83 years old and I have come to realize
that there is always more in life to learn. I just
started taking swimming lessons last year.
I ask a lot of questions during my
swimming lessons. You can drown yourself
with problems if you do not ask questions.
—Rosa Parks
Dear Mrs. Parks: A Dialogue with Today's Youth

• •

A hard head makes for a soft behind.
—*Traditional*

Wisdom does not come overnight.
—*Somalia*

Children are the wisdom of the nation.
—*Liberia*

Learn by others' mistakes because you do not
live long enough to make them all yourself.
—*Traditional*

• •

I'm three years older than the last time
I was here. That means I know ten times
as much as I did then. (Geeder)
Virginia Hamilton, Zeely

• •

LOYALTY

loyalty: constant devotion or allegiance; faithfulness.

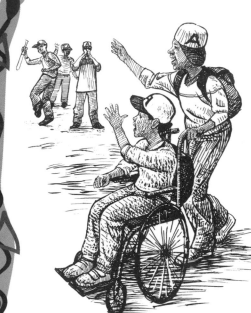

Often we don't appreciate the importance of loyalty. A loyal friend is someone who is dependable, trustworthy, and faithful. A loyal friend will stick by you through thick or thin. A loyal friend is always there when needed.

Have you ever needed an important favor from someone? A favor that would require a sacrifice? A loyal friend would be willing to make that sacrifice to help you.

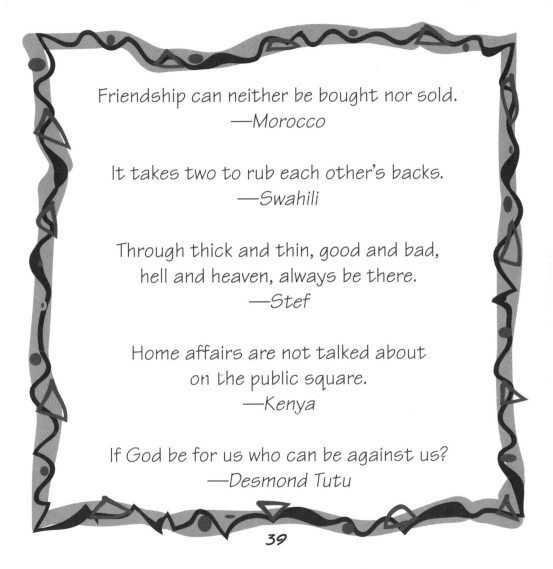

Friendship can neither be bought nor sold.
—Morocco

It takes two to rub each other's backs.
—Swahili

Through thick and thin, good and bad,
hell and heaven, always be there.
—Stef

Home affairs are not talked about
on the public square.
—Kenya

If God be for us who can be against us?
—Desmond Tutu

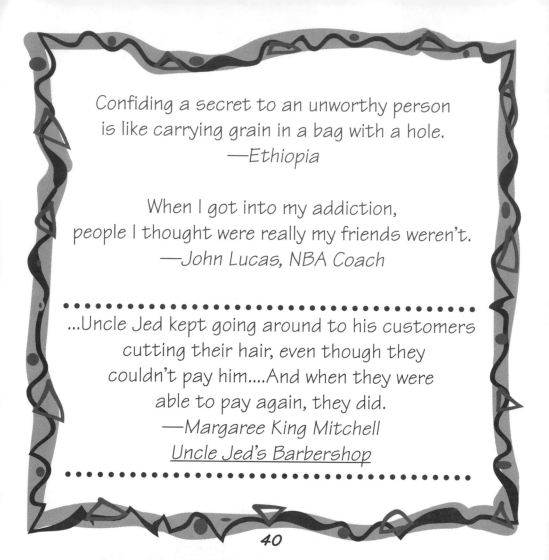

Confiding a secret to an unworthy person
is like carrying grain in a bag with a hole.
—*Ethiopia*

When I got into my addiction,
people I thought were really my friends weren't.
—*John Lucas, NBA Coach*

...Uncle Jed kept going around to his customers
cutting their hair, even though they
couldn't pay him....And when they were
able to pay again, they did.
—*Margaree King Mitchell*
<u>*Uncle Jed's Barbershop*</u>

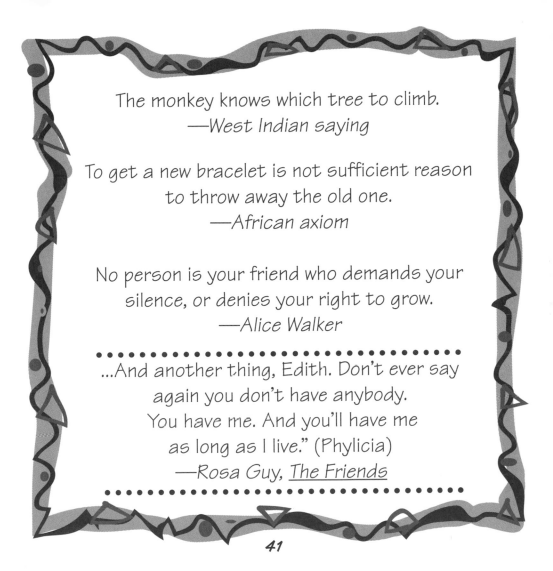

The monkey knows which tree to climb.
—*West Indian saying*

To get a new bracelet is not sufficient reason
to throw away the old one.
—*African axiom*

No person is your friend who demands your
silence, or denies your right to grow.
—*Alice Walker*

...And another thing, Edith. Don't ever say
again you don't have anybody.
You have me. And you'll have me
as long as I live." (Phylicia)
—*Rosa Guy, The Friends*

PATIENCE

patience: the ability to put up with hardship, pain, trouble or delay calmly and without complaint or anger.

Things don't always happen when we want them to. Many of us get angry and upset when they don't. If we are patient, we are willing to wait without getting distressed or anxious. We often make the wrong decisions when we are impatient or act in haste.

Do you rush someone else in your family who moves slower than you do? Maybe it is a grandparent or a younger brother or sister. How would you feel if they were impatient with you?

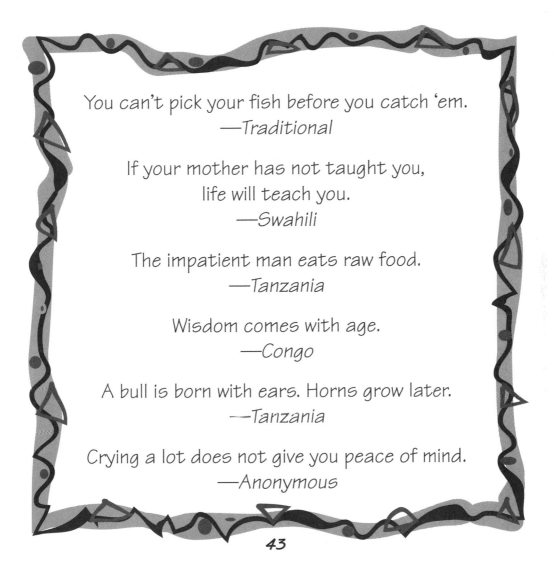

You can't pick your fish before you catch 'em.
—*Traditional*

If your mother has not taught you,
life will teach you.
—*Swahili*

The impatient man eats raw food.
—*Tanzania*

Wisdom comes with age.
—*Congo*

A bull is born with ears. Horns grow later.
—*Tanzania*

Crying a lot does not give you peace of mind.
—*Anonymous*

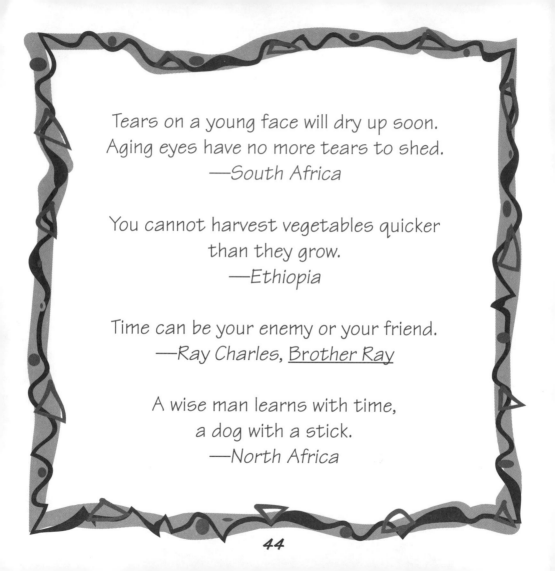

Tears on a young face will dry up soon.
Aging eyes have no more tears to shed.
—*South Africa*

You cannot harvest vegetables quicker
than they grow.
—*Ethiopia*

Time can be your enemy or your friend.
—*Ray Charles, <u>Brother Ray</u>*

A wise man learns with time,
a dog with a stick.
—*North Africa*

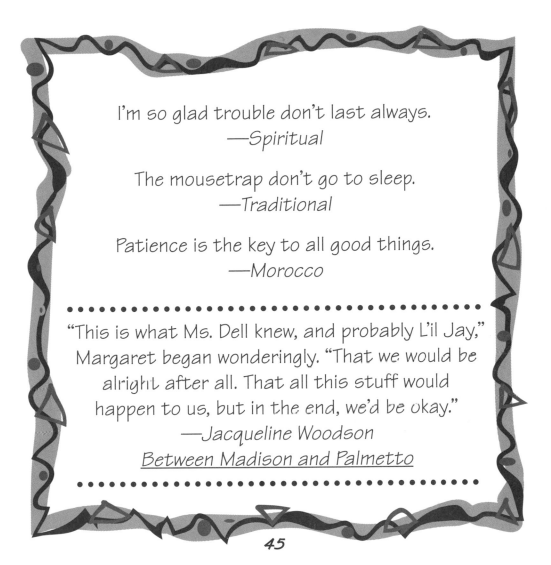

I'm so glad trouble don't last always.
—*Spiritual*

The mousetrap don't go to sleep.
—*Traditional*

Patience is the key to all good things.
—*Morocco*

• •

"This is what Ms. Dell knew, and probably L'il Jay,"
Margaret began wonderingly. "That we would be
alright after all. That all this stuff would
happen to us, but in the end, we'd be okay."
—*Jacqueline Woodson*
<u>*Between Madison and Palmetto*</u>

• •

RESPONSIBILITY

responsibility: the ability to distinguish between right and wrong and to think and act rationally.

A person who is responsible is trustworthy and dependable. A responsible person can be counted on to do the right thing. People often look to those who are responsible to take on big challenges, and to be leaders.

If a teacher puts you in charge of a special project can you be depended on to complete it? Do you do the chores your parents ask you to do? If you are responsible, the answers are "yes."

Use your head every day.
Use medicine only in time of need.
—*Yoruba*

When you go to the donkey house
don't talk about ears.
—*Jamaica*

What goes around comes around.
—*Traditional*

I have walked that long road to freedom.
But I can rest only for a moment, for with
freedom comes responsibilities; and I dare not
linger, for my long walk is not ended.
—*Nelson Mandela*

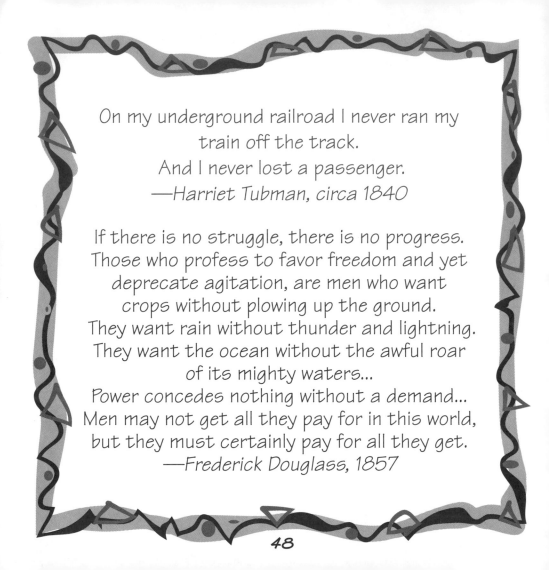

On my underground railroad I never ran my train off the track.
And I never lost a passenger.
—Harriet Tubman, circa 1840

If there is no struggle, there is no progress. Those who profess to favor freedom and yet deprecate agitation, are men who want crops without plowing up the ground.
They want rain without thunder and lightning. They want the ocean without the awful roar of its mighty waters...
Power concedes nothing without a demand... Men may not get all they pay for in this world, but they must certainly pay for all they get.
—Frederick Douglass, 1857

One good deed deserves another.
—Aesop

Went to the rock to hide my face.
Rock cried out "no hiding place!"
—Lyrics, Black Spiritual

I am glad to see that men are getting their rights,
but I want women to get theirs, and while
the water is stirring I will step into the pool.
—Sojourner Truth

• •

From nine years of trial and error, I had
learned that punishment was always less
severe when I poured out the whole truth
to Mama on my own before she heard
anything from anyone else. (Cassie)
Mildred D. Taylor, _Roll of Thunder, Hear My Cry_

• •

TRUST

trust: to have faith or confidence;
to be honest, truthful and reliable.

Can you be trusted?
If a friend tells you a very
important secret can you
keep it? A person who can be
trusted is reliable, honest,
and dependable.
Suppose a classmate at
school loses a sum of money
and you find it. Would you
give it back? Would you keep
it? A trustworthy person
would give the money back to
the rightful owner.
Are your trustworthy?

Fishes swim towards those of the same size.
—*Yoruba*

One man you can trust is better
than an army of cowards.
—*Egypt*

The best way to keep a secret is
not to tell it to anyone.
—*Swahili*

A liar has a short life.
—*Egypt.*

Does the mosquito thank you for your blood!?
—*Swahili*

Only a fool believes everything he is told.
—*Kunama*

In the bush, "trust" no one you do not know.
—*Alex Haley*

You better not shake hands with a crawfish.
—*Traditional*

Every good-bye don't mean I've gone.
Every shut eye ain't sleep.
—*Traditional*

When your hand is in leopard's mouth,
be careful how you pull it out.
—Liberia

We decide our affairs, then rest them with God.
—Jabo

The measure of a man is in the lives he's touched.
—Earnie Banks

• •

Mike put his arms around his mother.
Maybe he could make her understand.
He hugged her hard.
That's what she had done—hugged him.
—Sharon Bell Mathis
<u>The Hundred Penny Box</u>

• •

WORK

work: to do; act; physical or mental effort exerted to do or to make something.

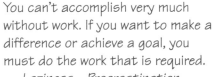

You can't accomplish very much without work. If you want to make a difference or achieve a goal, you must do the work that is required.

Laziness. Procrastination. Giving up. These keep us from putting forth the effort necessary to get things done. Frederick Douglass and Sojourner Truth knew that it would take a lot of work to abolish slavery. Their efforts helped put an end to that awful system that kept millions of Black people in chains.

You must work hard to achieve your goal, too, whether it is a small task or a big job.

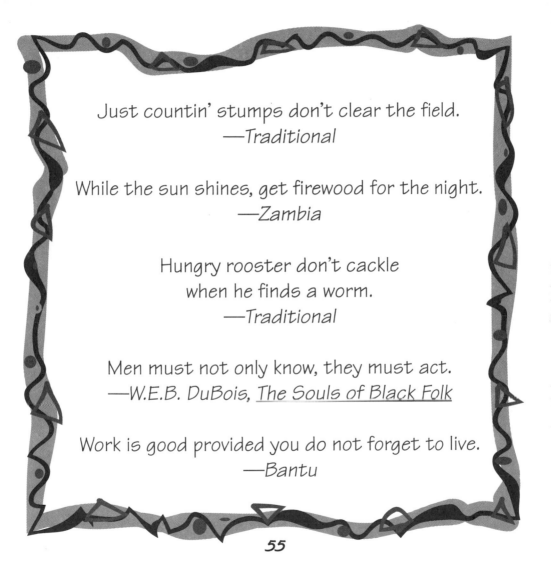

Just countin' stumps don't clear the field.
—*Traditional*

While the sun shines, get firewood for the night.
—*Zambia*

Hungry rooster don't cackle
when he finds a worm.
—*Traditional*

Men must not only know, they must act.
—*W.E.B. DuBois, The Souls of Black Folk*

Work is good provided you do not forget to live.
—*Bantu*

A lazy man will work 'til easy work comes his way.
—Zambia

Talking 'bout fire doesn't boil the pot.
—Traditional

You can't sit on the bucket and
draw water at the same time.
—Traditional

An empty wagon makes the most noise.
—Traditional

The seeker of drunkenness will
one day have enough.
The seeker of knowledge will never have enough.
—Swahili

The harvest truly is plenteous
but the labourers are few.
Matthew 9:37
The Original African Heritage Bible

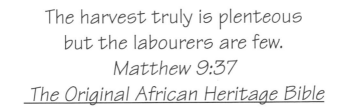

Sojourner Truth turned to the men who were
seated behind her. "Look at me!"... Her dark arm
was muscular, made strong by hard work. "I have
ploughed. And I have planted. And I have gathered
into barns. And no man could head me." She
paused again and asked this time in a whisper.
"And ain't I a woman?"
—Patricia C. McKissack and Fredrick McKissack
Sojourner Truth Ain't I A Woman?

WISDOM FOR PARENTS

The son of a fool will not become a chief.
—*Kunama*

Your child doesn't belong to you, and you must
prepare your child to pick up the burden
of his life long before the moment when
you must lay your burden down.
— James Baldwin, *The Devil Finds Work*

Do not forbid your son to eat his porridge hot:
his burnt tongue will teach him what you can't.
— *Tetela*

If you learn it while young, you can do it when old.
— *South Africa*

Mother is Gold.
— *Yoruba*

Without children the world would come to an end.
— Swahili

Racism is easy to see, hard to prove,
impossible to deny.
— Anonymous

(God) did give us children
to make (our) dreams seem worthwhile.
— Lorraine Hansberry, "A Raisin in the Sun"

We have rarely been encouraged and equipped
to appreciate the fact that the truth works,
that it releases the spirit and that
it is a joyous thing.
—Toni Cade Bambara

NGUZO SABA
The Seven Principles of Kwanzaa

UMOJA: UNITY
Let nothing and nobody break your spirit.
Let the unity in the comunity remain in tact.
—*Jesse Jackson, 1989*

KUJICHAGULIA: SELF-DETERMINATION
Don't let your enemies get in the way of your work.
— *Hausa*

UJIMA: COLLECTIVE WORK AND RESPONSIBILITY
Even the sharpest knife-blade
cannot carve its own handle.
—*Anonymous*

UJAMAA: COOPERATIVE ECONOMICS
God lent us his property here so that we too
could lend what we have to our neighbor.
— *Swahili*

NIA: PURPOSE
If you never reach, you're never going
to grab what you're after.
— *Traditional*

KUUMBA: CREATIVITY
Cease to be a drudge, seek to be an artist.
— *Mary McLeod Bethune*

IMANI: FAITH
A man can get along if he has faith in the good-
ness of other people ... and believes in himself.
— *Roy Wilkins*

Acknowledgments

About the Editors and Illustrator

Cheryl and Wade Hudson are founders of Just Us Books, Inc. and are creators of the AFRO-BETS[R] KIDS series. Together they have written, edited and published over three dozen books for children. They are currently compiling a family anthology entitled *In Praise of Our Fathers and Our Mothers*.

Anna Rich has illustrated a number of children's books including *Annie's Gifts, Joshua's Mask, Saturday at the New You* and *Cleveland Lee's Beale Street Band*. Ms. Rich is a graduate of Rhode Island School of Design. She lives in Elmont, New York, with her husband, Harry.

The editors gratefully acknowledge the following authors and publishers for permission to reproduce extracts quoted in this work:

From BETWEEN MADISON AND PALMETTO by Jacqueline Woodson. Copyright (c) 1995 by Jacqueline Woodson. Reprinted with permission of Bantam Doubleday Dell.

From THE BLACK SNOWMAN by Phil Mendez. Copyright (c) 1989 by Phil Mendez. Reprinted by permission of Scholastic Inc.

From CIRCLE OF GOLD by Candy Dawson Boyd. Copyright (c) 1984 by Candy Dawson Boyd. Reprinted by permission of Scholastic Inc..

From CORNROWS by Camille Yarbrough, copyright 1979. Reprinted by permission of The Putnam & Grosset Group.

Reprinted with the permission of Atheneum Books for Young Readers, an imprint of Simon & Schuster Children's Publishing Division. From THE DANCING GRANNY. Copyright (c) 1977 Ashley Bryan.

From DEAR MS. PARKS: A DIALOGUE WITH TODAY'S YOUTH. Copyright (c) 1996 by Rosa Parks. Reprinted with permission of Lee and Low Books, Inc.

From THE FRIENDS by Rosa Guy. Copyright (c) 1973 by Rosa Guy. Repinted with permission of Bantam Doubleday Dell.

From THE HUNDRED PENNY BOX by Sharon Bell Mathis. Copyright (c) 1975 by Sharon Bell Mathis, text. Used by permission of Viking Penguin, a division of Penguin Books USA Inc.

Exerpted from ROLL OF THUNDER, HEAR MY CRY by Mildred D. Taylor. Copyright (c) 1976 by Mildred D. Taylor, text. Used by permission of Dial Books for Young Readers, a division of Penguin Books USA Inc.

From SCORPIONS, copyright (c) 1988 by Walter Dean Myers. Reprinted with permission of HarperCollins Publishers.

From SOJOURNER TRUTH: AIN'T I A WOMAN? by Patricia C. McKissack and Fredrick McKissack. Copyright (c) 1992 by Patricia McKissack. Reprinted by permission of Scholastic Inc.

"the drum" from SPIN A SOFT BLACK SONG by Nikki Giovanni. Copyright (c) 1971, 1985 by Nikki Giovanni. Reprinted by permission of Farrar, Straus and Giroux, Inc.

From THE TIGER WHO WORE WHITE GLOVES copyright (c) 1974 by Gwendolyn Brooks. Reprinted with permission of Third World Press. All rights reserved.

Reprinted with the permission of Simon & Schuster Books for Young Readers, an imprint of Simon & Schuster Children's Publishing Division. From THE TRAIN TO LULU'S by Elizabeth Fitzgerald Howard. Text copyright (c) 1988 Elizabeth Fitzgerald Howard.

Reprinted with the permission of Simon & Schuster Books for Young Readers, an imprint of Simon & Schuster Children's Publishing Division from UNCLE JED'S BARBERSHOP by Margaree King Mitchell. Text copyright (c) 1992 Margaree King Mitchell.

Except from YELLOW BIRD AND ME. Copyright (c) 1886 by Joyce Hansen. Reprinted by permission of Clarion Books/Houghton Mifflin Co. All rights reserved.

Reprinted with the permission of Simon & Schuster Books for Young Readers, an imprint of Simon & Schuster Children's Publishing Division from ZEELY by Virginia Hamilton. Text copyright (c) 1967 Virginia Hamilton.

Special thanks to: Kelli Gary, Tonya Martin, Katura Hudson, Stephan Hudson, Marquita Guerra and Veronica Freeman Ellis, for their editorial assistance and research. Thanks also to Carol T. Jenkins of Jenkins Graphics for the cover and book design.